The Guide
To Identify
The DL Guy

Chloe Berringer

outskirtspress
DENVER, COLORADO

Acknowledgments

First and foremost, I'd like to thank and acknowledge my mom. You know who you are ma... Also special thanks to the creator for giving me my mom, my family & friends. I would like to thank my few good guy friends who openly identify as homosexual and played a part in the research that helped me create my guide. I also want to say I support them and their choices I respect the LGBT community. I am not looking to bash, but this issue has taken a turn for the worst. It can only get worst not better if we ignore it. Be aware, be careful, don't be afraid to ask questions, because those questions, and your heightened awareness could keep you out of harm's way, protect your heart from heartache, and save you from unnecessary pain.

I hope this guide reaches all women who are interested in the opposite sex, because these men on the down low keeping this part of their life a secret. All women must take heed, read the guide to be well informed. Take in the information, and watch out for these kind of men with these kind of secrets.

Contents

The Beginning of the End

This is a guide to help identify the DL guy; this is an issue that should be exposed. This guide will help inform women who don't know, and never suspected that this could be a problem that is silently plaguing their lives. The problem that I am referring to is DL-down low men; which are men who lead heterosexual lives with wives, girlfriends. But then on the Down Low, also have a sexual appetite for homosexual encounters, all while being in a relationship with a woman who isn't informed about their sexual orientation. That is because these men are being DL- Deceitful Liars regarding all their sexual preferences.

This guide will go in depth about the sites on the Internet where DL HETEROSEXUAL MEN can go on to become members, in order to gain access to other men who are on these sites to find men to have sexual relations with. In today's society women have to be aware of the men they are in relationships with because this issue doesn't discriminate. In this guide I am going to provide some of the websites you can go on to, along with some information. Because I want all women to become aware, be cautious, and stay protected. By going on these websites you can see what I seen, so that if you suspect your partner is leading a double life he just might be on one of these sites. Hmm I don't know but I have seen a lot of pictures of men who I would have never suspected, would have expected, and was in shock.

I feel like this information should be shared it's been an old problem that has managed to take spotlight, then its fizzles and fades in the darkness. Meanwhile these DL men aren't telling their female partners that they identify as a bisexual man instead of heterosexual man. I am not writing this guide to bash, disrespect, or slander any men. These men probably do deserve one out of the three consequences, because these DL men don't have the right to keep their sexual orientations a secret from their spouse, mate, or significant other.

I know they say if you look for something bad, you just might find it. In my personal opinion I would want to know something about my man being a low down, lying, trifling cheater living foul double life. I think that it's something that keeps getting exposed, and has not been taken seriously that is why these men feel invincible.

Every day more and more websites are being created, with more and more men adding their pictures and profiles, meanwhile beginning the search for men to have sex with. Every woman who finds this out is disgusted, sad, angry, scared, and confused as to why these men want to lead these double lives. I don't have the answer for that question, and I don't claim to know why these men lie about being heterosexual.

I tried to ask some of these men why they are living these Double Lives, lying to their girlfriends and wives, all while they are sneaking around having sex with men. I also ask them why they don't share their feelings and encounters with the women in their lives, in order to give them the opportunity to choose if they want to continue in the relations. Well I haven't got an answer as of yet when I ask the men on this one hookup site they shut down their profile, and suspend their account.

I know why these men do this, it's because they know what they're doing is wrong, they know that the relationship is definitely would be over, they are ashamed, and they know that their secrets will be exposed to their peers, as well as their relatives. The lie that is their life would be exposed for the fraud it is, because now the guys he hangs out with may not approve of his new lifestyle, causing him to lose his male friends.

A lot of these men if not all of them are really selfish, self-centered, and deceitful. I say this solely based on fact, because these men know that the women, whom they are in relationships with would definitely not stay, if they knew the truth about their sexual orientations.

That truth is so ugly for a heterosexual female who has no clue that her man is living this double life. The truth is ugly and these men keep it a secret, sneaking around having sexual relations with men. These men are not confused they are not ashamed about coming out the closet. They just want to have sex with men behind their female companion's back, keeping this secret from their family, friends, coworkers, and spouses.

The Down Low man is keeping his sexual preference for male seeking male sexual encounters a secret from his female sexual partners, because the shame would be too much for him to endure. He is a coward, and deceitful so he knows that it would cause chaos in his life. This secret getting out would cause shame to his image; women would not ever want to be with him again unless she was into that. Which is not the case, and these men know that, this is why they are on the Down Low.

A lot of these men are really screw up especially the ones in the dating scene or in a relationship, I say this because I have seen profiles of men who openly admit to being married on the down low. Also I have seen men who have profiles on dating sites such as Tagged looking for women to meet, but also these same men have profiles on the sites for men who are seeking men such as Adam4Adam. Meanwhile while they are playing both sides, these men on the down low aren't disclosing their sexual encounters, or their preferences being interested in both men and women. They know that can't have it both ways, and this is one of the reasons why they keep this a secret from the women in their lives.

If and when this secret is exposed it will and should cause chaos in these men who lead these deceptive lives, with this huge deceitful lie. This secret causes so much destruction, pain, and can even cause health problems for all involved due to the increase in sexually transmitted diseases. As well as emotional problems for the woman that is caught in the web of lies, that is created when these men decide to have relations with both sexes.

The Reasons

I have many reasons for writing this guide, and I would like to start off by saying that my opinions, the data, and my research was not collected to disrespect or judged anyone who openly identifies themselves as being a part of the LGBT community. But I am really appalled, and I feel the truth should be exposed on men who act, play, portray, or say that they only identify their sexual orientation as being Heterosexual. There is an acronym for this kind of man DL; Down Low it should also be DL; Deceitful Liars what you classify as disgusting, disrespectful, lying ass selfish, scumbags.

In my opinion, I feel if a homosexual man is in secret that is fine, or coming out is cool too. I can even respect a Heterosexual man who realizes that they want to be with men, and informs his significant other of his preferred sexual orientation. Now that would be painful, and something to recover from, but it's being honest and true.

But a Heterosexual man who hides his homosexual tendencies from his female partner, then secretly searches for sexual encounters on the internet is a piece of shit. When a man is in a relationship with a woman, and she wholeheartedly, without shadow of a doubt, could never imagine the man she thought was heterosexual was in fact bisexual. That is one of the ultimate betrayals, very deceitful, not to mention extremely dangerous. The consequences of these actions are harmful, hurtful, and traumatic to the female's psyche, and their self-esteem. Men should be really careful because you reap what you sow, how could you want to deceive, harm, and hurt the person you love.

I am writing this guide to take you through the web of lies and deceit that I have uncovered with my investigation, and research. With all the information I have collected, I can try to help you identify some signs, and show you what websites to search. As well as informing all women as to what they should watch out for. Because with today's technology and the World Wide Web, even though it is used to make things easier, it also has made things somewhat more complicated. I say this because it's so many websites that cater to Down Low men looking to secretly hook up with homosexual men or other Down Low men.

Another reason as to why I have decided to do the research, discover all this depressing evidence, and write this guide. Because I met a girl when I was in my twenties names Donna, whose sister's marriage came to an end when she found out that her husband, and the father of her 2 kids. Whom she had been married to for 8 years was a DL man, and was actively sleeping with his best friend, who also was his best man at their wedding. The way she found out was the worst, because she was a stay a home mom the only resource she could rely upon was a private investigator whom she hired. After the first week the private investigator was confused as to why he was following her husband, especially after only witnessing what look to be just best friends hanging out, like guys do going to the gym together, to play pool, or having drinks at a local sports bar. But by the second week it seemed like a routine, up until he witnessed the best friend, and her husband check into a hotel two towns away staying for three hours. Needless to say the private investigator brought back photos, and she was devastated, I personally have never seen someone so distraught.

In society women think they only have to worry about other women sleeping with their men, but now they also have to worry about their men having sexually relations with men too.

These behaviors that these men are engaging in is one of the leading causes of sexually transmitted diseases running rampant especially HIV. This is an issue that doesn't discriminate against age, location, or race.

It is an issue that is causing many detrimental effects on society as a whole. Because the men on the DL lead these Double Lives, endangering the health and well-being of all parties involved.

I am shedding light on a very, very, very dark issue, which has been identified, but not fucking scrutinized. WHY? I don't know, logically you would think if most women don't want their man to sleep with another woman, then they definitely wouldn't want their man to sleep with another man that's it period!

I am a woman in my thirties, who hopes to meet my soulmate, get married, but with this epidemic of men wanted to be with women and men. Seeing what I have seen, and knowing what I know I am more aware, and definitely on guard. I also feel like and with all the many other obstacles that relationships face I wouldn't want this to ever be an issue that affected my life.

I have spoken to groups of women from different circles, and all walks of life, but when I ask these women if they would date a man who openly identified himself as being bisexual. The answers to that question from all of the women in those groups, whom identified themselves as being heterosexual, stated that they would absolutely not date a man that identified as being bisexual.

Then when I questioned 5 different women who identified themselves as being bisexual, and I asked them the same question; would you date a man who identified himself as being bisexual. The response from three out of five of the women was that it didn't make a difference, and they would date a man who identified himself as being bisexual.

Although a lot of these men aren't openly identifying themselves as being bisexual they are keeping it a secret, sneaking around, and doing unthinkable things with men. All the while their female companions, girlfriends, or wives aren't thinking that their men are having homosexual sexual trysts. The reasons are plentiful, and at the end day I feel like all women should be made aware of the situations going on in their relationships, even if their partner isn't going to keep them informed.

In addition to that it should be a must to having the right to know all the details regarding your partner's sexual preference or preferences. With these DL men not fessing up these women won't know because they are deceitful, and don't care about anyone but themselves. This factual information because if these DL men really cared about their female companions, girlfriends, or wives then they would be responsible, and divulged all the details regarding their sexual preference or preferences regardless of the consequences. Do we live in a society now where this is normal? No we don't if you ask a room full of women if they would have a problem with their mate, being a bisexual.

Mostly maybe even all women would agree that this is a

deal breaker, non-negotiable terms of the relationship. When women find out that their mate is cheating on them, it's damaging to their feelings. Now when a woman finds out that it's not a side chick that their partner has cheated on them with, but in fact it's a man.

That is the ultimate betrayal of the relationship, and now the women are exposed to all other effects of this differs but now women of today's society also have to worry about their men cheating on them with men, because men are living secretly as DL homosexual men. I think that a man that chooses that lifestyle should be forthcoming and honest with his partner.

I would want to know if I was in a relationship with a man, who I expected to be heterosexual. If he was participating in homosexual activities, then the relationship is over immediately.

Most women feel the same way as me period point blank. With this guide being the additional hard proof that this issue is real, bad, and it's not going to go away. You have to be aware, be careful, stay protected, and be smart about the men you become involved with.

Therefore, this guide will be a very informative source, so now all the ladies need to do is read this guide cover to cover. In addition, do your own research, review all my research, and of course now you have to ask. Please don't feel any type of way because it's not a disrespectful question, because I have seen countless amounts of pictures of men who are not out, and living a double life.

It's a disturbing truth, that has been an issue for quite some time. But its reality, and I rather seem a little blunt, asking the question, and aware, then to be in the unknown. News flash these Deceitful Liars, living these Double Lives on the Down Low aren't going to come out, and let their female partners in on their dirty secrets. These men don't want anyone to know, that is why they go out of their way to sneak around in computer land. Which leads to linking up in real life, and then they have sex with men behind the backs of their unsuspecting female partners.

I rather be alone then to be in a relationship with a man who actively or has ever fantasized about being with a man. We have so many odds against us as females, and now this is just another one to add to the list. I don't want to be with a man, in a relationship, maybe even married, and then I find out that the man I love is attracted, and having relations with men.

I feel like this the men who are exposed should be shamed, because they knew what they were doing was wrong. If they hadn't been exposed, then they weren't going to divulge this information to the women in their lives.

My Investigative Research

This is the meat of the guide I have DONE extensive research with the help of few good research regarding this matter. I am a nervous about dating now, because this issue is so real. I am a woman who is looking to find a man who has certain attributes, beliefs, and characteristics. We all have a list of our ideal man, so now I have to state on my list that I want: A healthy heterosexual male.... The reality is really real I found a couple of dozen sites for men who want to hook up with men even though they have women at home who think they are heterosexual. This is how you start you seeking out one of the sites that I mention below. Then you create a profile as a man, and then answer those questions that I told you about earlier. Then go through the step to become member, and then search in your country, state, and town. Watch how many men you will see on there that are not out of the closet, on the DL and are actively looking for a sex buddy, meanwhile their unsuspecting girlfriend, or wife sitting at home with this being the last thing on their mind. It is happening and I can name other websites on the

World Wide Web that I found while doing my research, here is a more in depth list:

1. DL Hookup
2. DL-Men-Only on Black Planet
3. Raw Nasty Fuckers
4. Craigslist; Erotic Svc- (which is now Personals) Men seeking men (MSM)
5. Just Us Boys
6. Shybi-guys
7. ICQ chatrooms for Bi-curious men
8. Bisexual playground
9. Sketchy Sex
10. Fuckbook
11. Straightguise
12. Manhunt.com
13. Thugs4thugs
14. DLBrothas
15. Mingle2
16. Downelink
17. Ourtime.com
18. Gaydating
19. Barebackrt
20. Adam4adam
21. GRINDR

That's just too name more than a few, there are also other methods to hook-up using Search engines, which have been hidden it in many different forms. All you have to do is word while searching online, such as searching bisexual men, male seeking male, bi-curious men, gay men straight men, straight men for gay men, parties for straight men to have sex with men, straight guys looking to have same sex fun, and straight guys bending over. The rising numbers of men searching out secret sexual relationships on these sites is alarming.

This one site in particular where I got a lot pertinent information is called "Adam4Adam" @ www.adam4adam.com there are around 100,000 - 150,00 male members logged on during any given Monday thru Saturday at all times. It's sad but out of those 100,000-150,000 men half of those members are DL men.

The website Adam4Adam.com is an online site that is very detailed in what questions they ask for the membership to obtain a profile. After becoming a member, you activate your profile, upload pics if you want to, and then gain access to seek out men to have sexual hook ups with.

Ladies if you want to go see for yourself then do the research yourself, follow the path, and find out after you gain access you will be able to see all those men.

The questions are asking the man about his physical appearance: age, height, weight, waist size, body type, hair color, and body hair. Their ethnicity, what he is into sexually, or how they ask "what he is looking for" with choices like: friendship, relationship, 1 on 1 sex, threesome/group sex, miscellaneous fetishes, and Cam2Cam sex. Also one of the questions asked was the size of his Penis, and if it cut or uncut.

What is your Sexual Role? Choices are bottom, top, versatile top, versatile bottom, oral, foreplay. Some of those term is self-explanatory the ones that you might not be familiar with are. A Bottom is a man who prefers to be at the bottom getting penetrated, a Top is a man who prefers to be on top doing the penetrating. A Versatile bottom is a man that is comfortable with a shared dominance in the intimate acts and he will be on top or on the bottom depending on the relationship. A versatile top is a man that is comfortable with a shared dominance, and he will either be on top or on the bottom depending on the relationships as well however sexually, enjoy being a top more than a bottom. One of the questions being asked on this online site in order to obtain a member profile on Adam4adam.com is are you OUT?

This means you have revealed that your sexual orientation & preference is homosexuality. The Choices to choose from are yes or no for example Out No means that they have not come out as being homosexual, and Out Yes means that the male member openly identifies as being homosexual.

Here are some more questions and terms that you may not be familiar with. Such as What scene you're into? Choices: alternate, casual, conservative, drag, jock, leather, military, punk, or trendy.

So if you aren't out of the closet you have the choice to show your pics or lock them. I also know that DL men are also on Backpage, Craigslist-erotic services; male seeking male. There are countless other websites that are for men looking to hookup NSA- No Strings Attached. If you don't believe me take a look for yourself. Play around with the words in any search engine for example straight men looking to hook up with men, men seeking men, straight men and gay men dating, and by searching the internet some of the sites that I named above were listed in the search.

Other terms to look out for are:

Cruising- on personal mean to be looking for a hook up

DDF- discreet disease free

DL – down low

Gay Curious- curious about one's homosexuality, curious to try

Homosexuality

Scene- for example if he is a jock, trendy, or casual

Bottom- he will allow himself to be penetrated

Top- he will on be the only one penetrating

TS- Transsexual meaning medically changing their gender

Transvestite (Tranny)-man that dresses up as a female

Transgender (TG) dresses as one gender, but still has the anatomy of their naturally born gender they are ex. Girl dresses as a man

Versatile – he will penetrate, and he will be penetrated

In order to gain access to the site to view these profiles, you have to the lingo, be able to answer the questions. These profiles are only able to be seen by members of this site. That is another indicator that when a man accesses this site, and creates a profile he cannot say it was a mistake. Because it is too detailed in the questioning regarding their sexual orientation, sexual preference, what they want on this site. In addition, it even allows the member to inform the other members if they are willing to entertain them at their place, or to be entertained at their place. These men can lock, unlock, the images that they uploaded which is usually nude, and pornographic photos of them. So we definitely know that finding this site, creating a profile to become a member, and uploading photos was done intentionally. When access is granted they have a large number of members to interact with from state to state, and country to country.

This is a vast amount of ground to cover when these men are trolling the site for sexual encounters with other Down Low men. Then this site also links to members who are having parties for down low men to attend. There are secret sex parties held at secret clubs, and other disclosed locations such as local area hotels. The websites are usually the link up to get invited to these secret sex parties, where men go to meet men to have sexual relations. There is a widespread epidemic of DL men orgies that cater to discreet men who lead double lives, sometimes traveling to different states for these exclusive clubs, and parties. The states where some of these parties are being held, which have been tracked down and observed by my sources are Atlanta, Baltimore, DC, Maryland, North Carolina, South Carolina, Philadelphia, and Virginia. The parties are usually given by these disguised entertainment companies, such as Mandingo Entertainment, which is linked to http://blackpassport.com/richmondparty1/. It's really graphic and shocking, because the content is homoerotic, and extremely X-rated so beware when you go to this site There are many other entertainment companies, not to mention the countless amounts of men that can post, host their own private parties in their local areas. Mandingo Entertainment is associated with www.Black Passport.com which isn't hard to find because they have many other events beside the 12-hour Fuck-A-Thon that they host for men to meet men to have sex with in hotel rooms. The hosts of these parties is charging $20.00 if tickets are purchased in advanced, $25.00 after 3am at the door to enter and participate. At these parties they also provide drinks, drugs, lube, and rubbers at these down low orgies. The parties move from state to state, and have a huge following of men who support them, and the men who attend are on the down low, bisexual or homosexual.

Here is one of the many fliers that circulated online advertising the party, hosted by the entertainment company that I mentioned above. This party was held at the Best Western Plus Holiday Sands Inn & Suites in Norfolk, Virginia on Friday, and Saturday on April 29th & 30th 2016, and it started at 11:59pm until 12pm. This party is where men who have sex with men go to meet secretly to hook-up sexually. I attempted to do a stakeout at this one but as you can see they are very discreet, and definitely don't allow women to attend these parties. They don't allow phones to be used at these events, but they do record the attendees who don't mind being recorded. I contacted the hotel where this party was being held and spoke to both a night manager and nighttime employee who were made aware of this party that they claimed they knew nothing about especially because this hotel caters to families and tourists because it is right directly near a beach.

Mandingo Adult Entertainment Presents

A Mandingo Party Where Men Go to Meet Men for the Black/Latin Thick Boi's Friday & Saturday,

April 29th & 30th 2016 @ the Best Western Plus Holiday Sands Inn & Suites 1330 E Ocean View Ave. room 237 in Norfolk, Virginia 23503

Party starts @ 11:59pm – 12 noon $25.00 @ the Door Don't park in the hotel parking lot there is plenty of parking on Sturgis St which is about half a block from the hotel... Use GPS or call this number 267-xxx-7273 for any questions or concerns. Come directly to the room do not go to the hotel front desk and ask questions about the party.

Here is another one of the many fliers that are circulated online advertising the party, hosted by the same entertainment company. This party was in Raleigh, Durham, and Greensboro, North Carolina on July 1st, 2nd, & 3rd, 2016, and the times of the parties are 11:59pm until 12 noon. This is where men who have sex with men go to meet secretly to hook-up sexually a three-day event going to the different cities listed. The men on this website are not actors they are some of the partygoers who attend, and as you can see participate at these parties.

Mandingo Adult Entertainment Presents

A Mandingo Party Where Men Go to Meet Men For the Black/Latin Thick Boi's Friday, Saturday, Sunday, July 1st, 2nd, & 3rd, 2016 In Raleigh – Durham – Greensboro, North Carolina 27707 for Independence Day Weekend 12-Hour-Fuck-A-Thons All Inclusive Party…$20.00 @ the Door/ $25.00 after 3am for each night advance tickets can be used July 1st, 2nd, or 3rd 2016 and can be exchanged for a later date if you miss the Party please bring exact change The Rules are come directly to the Hotel Room DO NOT CALL THE HOTEL FOR INFORMATION CALL US DIRECTLY 276-972-xxxx NO LOUD NOISE OUTSIDE THE HOTEL OR HANGING OUTSIDE IN CARS OR OTHERWISE…. GO IN OR OUT CALL US DIRECTLY FOR ROOM # AND EXPLICIT INSTRUCTIONS

Let me tell you something ladies, these men who were observed at these ill-sorted soirees don't look like men who have sex with men. So I myself was quite confused, because what we were taught to watch out for has completely taken a left turn. The men nowadays don't give off any homosexual vibes, exhibit no female tendencies, they are straight-acting, very masculine, and they aren't openly identifying themselves as being bisexual, or their sexual orientation preferences being men and women.

This issue can literally affect any and all women involved with a man, not saying to be paranoid, but you should do some investigating. It's safe to say you can't just go on the word of the man, because we know they aren't going to out themselves.

I will also say that this issue affects women who are between the ages of 18-72, and the reason I can use that age range is because I have seen 18, 28, 38, 48, 58, 60, and 72 yr. old men on these sites seeking secretive sexual relations with other men. So if you think this can't be a problem for you think again. This problem is affecting all women I will the first to tell I have seen white, black, Asian, Indian, all ethnicities on the websites looking to have sex with men. So no specific group of women is safe from this horribly perverse lifestyle that these men engage in. I say this because in my opinion it takes a real selfish person to say that they love their woman, but then go do something unspeakable. All while knowing that if she found out it would devastate her, and even if she doesn't know or never finds out, she would definitely disapprove.

I've seen men who openly admit to being married, in a relationship, or actively dating women. But yet and still these same men are also admitting that they are discreet, on the down low and don't want any drama as they sneak around in these chatrooms, on these sites, and at these events. All while their unsuspecting female partners are completely in the dark, and don't know a damn thing about their men and their double lives.

This is a problem that affects all women who are in marriages, relationships, or who are dating. There are so many men that are on these sites, and other sites who are purposely perpetrating fraud by allowing the women in their lives to believe that they only heterosexual. But in fact a lot of these men are bisexual or homosexual, and they are living a lie while they ac heterosexual.

No one can say they are confused about their sexual preference, because when you are truly confused you can't make a choice to create a profile on a site that caters to down low men seeking sexual fulfillment. Those are actions of someone who know exactly what they want, and how to go about getting it. No one should have the right to hide such a huge secret that would devastate, or harm their partner and the relationship. This issue causes a tremendous amount of pain and problems emotionally, mentally, and physically to all involved. Especially the women who don't know and find out the hard way, which is really no easy way to find out. But to be safe from harm's way, and not have contracted any kind STD's, the best thing is to find out, and not be in the dark.

The Research Regarding Health Risks

The dangers from the risky behaviors of these men who are on the down low jeopardizes the health, and sometimes lives of the women that they are in sexual relationships with. It is a devastating chain reaction for example: John has sex with his wife, but he also is having sex with Mark, who is having sex with Ralph, who also is having sex with Ramona, and Steve so on and so forth. Because these men are sexually active with both women and men it puts them at a higher risk.

Especially because some of these men aren't using protection when performing sexual acts with these random men, then they go home to the unsuspecting women in their lives and they aren't using protections with them either. I will be discussing the information that I reviewed on the CDC (Center for Disease Control) website, which is all public information that can be accessed online.

The links I will be providing to you in this guide will lead directly to the Center of Disease Control site, and they provide actual graphs and statistics of the data collected. The first link is: http://www.cdc.gov/std/sats14/msn.htm this is an article regarding the 2014 Sexually Transmitted Diseases Surveillance report. In this link it contains data that clearly states bisexual, gay, and other men who have sex with men (MSM) are at an increased risk to contract STDs compared to women and exclusively heterosexual men. Second link is: http://www.cdc.gov/mmwr/preview/mmwrhtml/mm5725a2.htm which is another article that is about the Trends in HIV/AIDS Diagnoses Among Men Who Have Sex with Men (MSM), and the data was collected from 33 states during the time period from 2001-2006. (*Center of Disease Control. Trends in HIV/AIDS diagnoses among men who have sex with men-33 States, 2000-2006. MMWR Morb Mortal Wkly Rep. 2008; 57:681-686*)

The next one is: http://cdc.gov/std/dstdp/ this link contains information about the special department that was created within the CDC, and it's called DSTDP its stands for Division of STD Prevention. This division is working hard to have long term impacts on STD prevention, and one of the four focus area that the DSTDP concentrates on is Men Who Have Sex with Men.

These are some numbers from data collected from an article off of the CDC website regarding MSM (men who have sex with men), so as of recent MSM are the most heavily affected group in the United States who have contracted the HIV virus. It was also stated by the CDC that in 2010, 63% accounted for all the new HIV infections, which were men who have sex with men (MSM), 25% heterosexual, 8% intravenous drug users, and 3% for intravenous drug users who have sex with men.

In addition, the CDC reports that the statistics show that all races were amongst these numbers, such as White (MSM) 11,200, African American (MSM) 10,600, Hispanic (MSM)

6,700. These are alarming number especially because it is reported that more than 3 million women are, or have been the wives or girlfriends of men who secretly have sex with other men. I will break it down again the DL (down low) man has a wife or girlfriend, but DL man is also having unprotected sex with a man on the side. That man on the side is having sexual relations with other people too, and the wife of the DL man might be creeping with her own sexual partners. NOW all it takes is for one of these people to be HIV positive.

Then you have a chain of people connected to an infected, then they continue to spread it amongst each other, and others with the unprotected and risky sexual encounters. I also read an article where it stated that from the studies performed that at least 20 percent of all gay men in America are in heterosexual marriages. It isn't just HIV, even though that is the worst STD you can contract, because it has no cure, and can kill you.

But there are other STDs that are being tracked by the CDC, such as Chlamydia, Gonorrhea, and Syphilis. A system was created to track these other STDs, which was named the STD Surveillance Network (SSUN). This program has 42 Sexually Transmitted Disease Clinics within 12 jurisdictions, which are Alabama, Baltimore, California, Chicago, Colorado, Connecticut, Louisiana, New York, Philadelphia, San Francisco, and Virginia) and they are responsible surveilling these STD statistics, collecting data, interpreting, managing, and reporting disease information.

They are also responsible for detecting and monitoring the trends of the prevalence of STD amongst MSM (men who have sex with men), and who also identify themselves as being bisexual or homosexual. I am so sad when thinking that it's going to be very hard for the younger generations to procreate, when there are going to be so many people infected with various curable or non-curable sexually transmitted diseases.

All these articles, graphs, and statistics can be reviewed later by accessing the CDC website http://www.cdc.gov so you can read them all in entirety.

Here is another link: http://www.cdc.gov/std/stats14/std-trends-508.pdf regarding the CDC Fact Sheet regarding "The Reported STDs in the United States 2014 National Data for Chlamydia, Gonorrhea, and Syphilis". This fact sheet summarizes the data collected in 2014 regarding the trends that cause the alarming increase in Sexually Transmitted Diseases being transmitted to men between the ages of 15 – 24 years of age. The data shows that MSM (men who sex with men) are the among the group who are burden by the increase in new cases reported. *CDC. Sexually Transmitted Diseases Treatment Guidelines, 2015. MMWR 2015 Jun 5; 64(RR-03);1-137)*

The Signs

There aren't really a lot of signs because a woman wouldn't knowingly date a man who has various sexual preferences if that wasn't something she was either into or okay with. Really just being a computer literate individual can help you to be proactive in checking, and ensuring that your man isn't involved in this kind of sorted affairs. Especially because a lot of this interaction starts from the computer, with all the accessibility in chat rooms, classified ads Back Page, Craigslist, and also membership required sites some are free some aren't. The sites make it easy for these men to carry on their secretive double lives. Because they don't advertise, nor do they make it easy to access you must create a profile. They aren't advertising like the social media website or popular dating websites. If you don't know what to look for you will surely overlook it.

Also if your iPad, iPhone, laptop, or desktop is always on private browser then that is suspicious internet activity. In addition, on those same items above, if the history or cookies are always cleared, or deleted. That is definitely suspicious behavior to clear all search history, and should raise some red flags. Because usually when we search the Internet we don't clear the cache, or delete browser history. Look for the photo vaults because those are discreet applications that allow photos to be hidden and protected by password. Now photo vaults have come a long way some Applications are camouflaged as a calculator where you then enter a password to gain access to photos. Such Apps are very easily purchased on all smartphones and other devices.

Again there aren't any real specific concrete signs just be aware, and ask the question don't worry about coming off rude. In today's society it's a question that should be asked, which is have you ever slept with a man before. As well as the next question that needs to be asked is have you ever felt attracted to a man before ever in your life. Now you're most likely not going to get an honest answer from these men, and I say this because from my research on these websites these DL men say they are the DL (Down Low), they locked their pictures, and they secretly have sexual relationships with men they meet on these websites.

Not trying to stir up paranoia, but with the alarming rate of heterosexual men seeking men do your research, be aware, and go with your gut. Remember ladies trust your intuition sometimes we see red flags, and for the sake of not being alone we put our blinders on. Therefore, for the women who live with their men check the computers, for example check the temporary internet files, and make CTRL + H your friend checks the browser history.

That's one signs to look out for if the browser history is empty this means that the person who used the computer last is deleting it on purpose. Aha what are they hiding, well those are suspicious behaviors, and should be watched closely. Also if your man is too touchy feely, or has increasing suspicious nonverbal communication with other men who aren't related to him, such as long hugs, looking up and down, staring at man too long. Those are red flags that should not be ignored, and other signs to be on the lookout for are if your man exchanges contact information with random men, who you know no prior meeting of and begins to have a lot of non-business related phone calls with strange men. In addition, an increased amount of new male friends who you have never met or heard about before

Just be aware, and if you sense something strange or weird then ask, because you have that right. Just don't expect any heart to heart confessions, this is a secret that they go out of their way to hide, it's no way to sugar coat it. In addition, there is no repairing a relationship after this secret is exposed. This means that you will have to find out on your own by reading this guide you have a fighting chance to know what to look for, and where to look for it at.

Pictures, Profile, Proof

Because of copyright laws I can't show you pictures of these men who are on the down low trolling this site for men to have sexual relations with. But I will show you examples of the profiles that I have seen with my own eyes. I will not be able to show you the exact screenshots of photos that I captured from this website while obtaining the information that is inside of this guide. But I will offer an email that all the readers will be allowed to subscribe too, this subscription will direct you to an auto responder that will allow you to see exactly what I could not print in this guide. This is the only way I can show you exactly what I saw, and the names of the actual website that I obtained all my information from. I will also be able to show you some of the questions that were asked in order to obtain a profile on this site. I will show a lot in this part of the book so that you can read the profiles, get familiar with the lingo because this is what these men are looking for on this website. Also along with these profiles these men are able to upload photos, and lock or unlock these photos whenever they want to. This website allows these men on the Down Low to literally put a lock on their photos so that any or all members are unable to be see them, unless the member unlocks them willingly.

Here is the first sample profile of one of the members:

USA – VIRGINIA - HAMPTON ROADS - NORFOLK

26, 6'2", 195LB, 34W MUSCULAR, BLACK, SHAVED BODY, MIX. **LOOKING FOR FRIENDSHIP, RELATIONSHIP, CAM2CAM, 1-ON-1 SEX.**

BORED...UP FOR CHATTING AND MEETING. NOT INTO DRAMA OR BS. I LIKE VIDEO GAMES, THEME PARKS.

SCENE CASUAL, **OUT NO**, SMOKE SOCIALLY, DRINK SOCIALLY, DRUGS NO, ZODIAC GEMINI.

8.5", CUT, VERSATILE, SAFE SEX ONLY, HIV NEGATIVE. PREFER MEETING AT: YOUR PLACE.

This is 26-year-old black man, who is 195lbs, with a 34" waist that IS NOT OUT OF THE CLOSET. This man is looking for a friendship, 1-on-1 sex, Cam2Cam, or a relationship with a man. He is a versatile DL man who has an 8.5" cut penis, is also HIV negative, and only into safe sex. He smokes, and drinks socially, and he enjoys playing video games. This 26-yr-old Down Low versatile (meaning he can take it or give it) man who is in Norfolk, Virginia, and prefers to travel to meet at the place of the male member.

OKAY take a deep breath it gets worst there were so many profiles that had the OUT NO Status in their profile bios. The ages, race, and locations were all different these men are all over you just don't know it could be your man, or your friends man. This website caters to people in all 52 states, and it also is available for men in other countries.

These men on this website can search in their local area or they can travel and search for members in other areas you have some men that are traveling and they search for the area that they are visiting.

Here is the second sample profile of another member:

USA – VIRGINIA - PORTSMOUTH

39, 6'2" 247LB, 36W, AVERAGE, BLACK, SOME BODY HAIR, MIX. LOOKING FOR: 1-ON-1 SEX, GROUP SEX, FRIENDSHIP.

I AM DISCREET DISEASE FREE LOOKING FOR FRIEND'S WITH BENEFITS ONLY

SCENE CASUAL, OUT NO, SMOKE SOCIALLY, DRUGS NO, ZODIAC PISCES

8.5", UNCUT, VERSATILE/TOP, SAFE SEX ONLY, HIV NEGATIVE. PREFER MEETING AT: YOUR PLACE

This is a 39-year-old, black man who is 6'2" 247 lbs. with a 36" waist average body frame with some body hair. This member is looking for friends with benefits only, who he can have group sex, 1-on-1 sex with. He is a Versatile and Top (meaning he can be penetrated or he can penetrate during anal sex, but he enjoys penetrating) man with an 8" uncut penis. He is in Portsmouth, Virginia and is willing to travel to your place.

USA – HAMPTON ROAD – VIRGINIA BEACH

47, 5'10" 186lb, 36W, MUSCULAR, BLACK, SOME BODY HAIR, LATINO LOOKING FOR: FRIENDSHIP, 1-ON-1 SEX, 3SOME (THREESOMES)/GROUP SEX.

LOVE A DOMINATING MAN, WHO IS MASCULINE, VERBAL AND VERY AGGRESSIVE. I AM ALSO INTO ROLE PLAYING AND SENSUALWRESTLING.

SCENE JOCK, OUT NO, SMOKE NO, DRINK OCCASSIONALLY, DRUGS SOCIALLY, ZODIAC AQUARIUS.

7.5", UNCUT, BOTTOM, SAFE SEX ONLY, HIV NEGATIVE
PREFER MEETING AT: MY PLACE

This is a 47-year-old Latino man that is 5'10 186lb with a muscular build. This member is into Threesome, Group sex, also looking for a friendship, 1-on-1 sex, role playing, and sensual wrestling. This member is a Bottom (which means he only wants to be penetrated when engaging in anal sex), he also is into the Jock scene, with a 7.5" Cut penis, also is HIV Negative, resides in Virginia Beach, Virginia willing to entertain members at his place. This is sad I know you are feeling dizzy just like did. I am going to show you a couple more sample profiles that I read. But when I tell you I seen a lot of profiles, I have personally seen at least 20,000 with my own eyes this website has up 110,000 men online on any given weekend.

Some of these men that have profiles are openly identifying themselves as being homosexually OUT YES, but it's not that many most of the profile I have come across are of men who are OUT NO, on the down low, and not out of the closet. This means they are actively dating, or are in relationships with women who don't have a clue.

Here is yet another man who has a profile, and his isn't even old enough to buy alcohol and at a young tender age of 20 he is into this:

USA - VIRGINIA – SUFFOLK

20, 6'1", 210LB, 34W. ATHLETIC, WHITE BUZZED BODY LOOKING FOR FRIENDSHIP, ORAL, JERKING OFF TOGETHER, 3SOMES.

SEEKING MASCULINE MEN ONLY GYM BUDDY IF POSSIBLE

SCENE JOCK, OUT NO, SMOKE YES, DRINK OCCASIONALLY, DRUGS NO, ZODIAC SAGITTARIUS.

6.5", CUT, VERSATILE, SAFE SEX ONLY, HIV NEGATIVE

Here is the last profile of a man who has a total of five pictures, which is also a free feature on the website. However, if the member decides that he wants to upload more than five photos, then he has to arrange payment to the website to do so. I can't expose any of this man's photos, I can tell you what I seen, and I will describe it in detail so let me warn you because the photos were X-rated, nasty, and raunchy. First off there were two pictures of his penis, 2 of his buttock being spread apart, and one photo of his face. Now when I first came across this man's profile only the text could be read and seen. Because his five pictures had been locked, but with the help of my friend who assisted me in my research began to converse with this member via direct message he unlocked all his photos for us to view and was willing to meet at a hotel (public place).

49, 5′9″, 210lb, 40W, LARGE, WHITE SOME BODY HAIR, LOOKING FOR: FRENDSHIP, RELATIONSHIP, 1-ON-1 SEX, 3SOMES, GROUP SEX, AND MISC FETISH- FISTING

SCENE MILITARY, OUT NO, SMOKE NO, DRINK NO, DRUGS NO, ZODIAC TAURUS

8″, CUT VERSATILE/ BOTTOM HIV NEGATIVE AS OF 2/2016 LIKE TO BAREBACK, LOVE ORAL PREFER MEETING AT: PUBLIC PLACE

This same man is looking for a friendship, relationship, 1-on-1 sex, 3somes, group sex, and he is also into Miscellaneous Fetishes; Fisting which involves a hand being balled into a fist, and then inserted into the anus. He likes to bareback that mean he doesn't like to use condoms.

I wanted to give my all in this guide for the most part I have given it my all, yet I still have more to give so if you want the rest of it... Then subscribe to the get the rest for Free

@ http://eepurl.com/b1ta3b so after you read this guide you will get an eyeful of what I seen. By visiting this link above and subscribing to receive the information that could not be included.

Recovering after the
Secret is Revealed

Picking up the pieces after you find out this terrible information, which is that the man you're in a loving relationship with is having sex with men. That's a huge pill to swallow; I have never experienced this turmoil personally. However, in my opinion, and this is based solely on my opinion I would let him know that I know, but not in a confrontational manner. Because the emotions will be intense I would then remove myself from situation for example if we lived together I would move out, and if we had kids I would also move them out too. I would go to my mom's and tell her these horrible secrets about him that were exposed show her the proof because I would be in shock so I would need another person to help me process it. The next thing to do is to make an emergency appointment with my gynecologist, and have the entire test performed to check for STD's.

I might even want to see a psychologist, because depending on how serious the relationship is, whether this man is your boyfriend, husband, or the father of your child. I think that talking to someone that will listen, who doesn't know you or him, such as an unbiased qualified professional to help process the situation. Due to all of the mixed emotions I wouldn't recommend confronting the situation until you spoke to someone.

I would pray for strength; I mean lots of strength because you will need every bit of strength you can muster. Because you will be beat down emotionally, and mentally due to the traumatic shocking things that you have discovered about the man you love. I watch my friend's sister almost lose her mind, I can't even blame her because I have never been in this situation. I think counseling helped get her back to a functioning capacity, being allowed to talk to an unbiased person whom you feel no judgement. Because this issue isn't the fault of the women, it is all the man's fault.

Forgiveness probably would be immediate, but that would be fine because when this coward is exposed he is going to go running trying to get away as far as he can. That's one thing that had me so confused how a man could be so careless with the feelings of his wife or girlfriend. Not once do these men on the down low think while they are performing these sexual acts with these men, how this would destroy the ladies in their life.

The best advice to give would be, to get as far away from this man as you can, because a man that can do this to you while telling you he loves you. This man is a nut case, because this is the most severe type of betrayal. He doesn't care about you at all, don't be conned by him saying that this won't happen again, it was a one-time thing. That is a lie, a deceitful disgusting lie which should be taken at face value would he be so sorry if you didn't find out and expose him, because they aren't going to tell you. The relationship is no more, it is nothing it's over, over, really over.

I would pray for the strength to be strong in this time of struggle, because I have seen how devastating this was when a woman I knew found out that her husband was on the down low. I watched someone who I considered to be strong fall completely apart from the bottom to the top literally almost lost her mind, neglecting herself physically, and was shattered emotionally. I didn't have any advice for her due my lack of experience I have never gone through something so traumatizing before. I did watch her slowly recover in time with the help of her family, friends with a lot counseling from a professional.

I pray for the women who were devastated from reading this guide, if it applies you have to pick up you pieces and take the proper precautions to make sure you recover. So don't go off into a bitter tyrant, because things can only get worse if you deal with this issue under distress or on in irrational state of mind. So I repeat this twice over Leave him Alone, Remove yourself from the man who has been exposed for being a Down Low Man Who Has Sex with Men Deceitfully lying to you while in a relationship.

www.ingramcontent.com/pod-product-compliance
Lightning Source LLC
Chambersburg PA
CBHW050350290526
45785CB00006B/2718